LOL JOKES

SAN FRANCISCO

I0801511

arcadia
CHILDREN'S BOOKS

CRAIG YOE!

Published by Arcadia Children's Books
A Division of Arcadia Publishing
Charleston, SC
www.arcadiapublishing.com

First published 2021

Manufactured in the United States

ISBN 978-1-4671-9844-8

Library of Congress Control Number: 2021938357

All images used © Shutterstock.com; p. 18-19 Daily Travel Photos/Shutterstock.com; p. 26 ChameleonsEye/Shutterstock.com; pp. 40, 64 (top right) Sundry Photography/Shutterstock.com; pp. 46, 50 Tada Images/Shutterstock.com; p. 46 KURLIN_CAfE/Shutterstock.com; p. 47 Willrow Hood/Shutterstock.com; p. 48 meunierd/Shutterstock.com; p. 60-61 Everett Collection/Shutterstock.com; p. 64 (left) FiledIMAGE/Shutterstock.com; p. 64 (bottom right) Anton_Ivanov/Shutterstock.com; p. 90 eddie-hernandez.com/Shutterstock.com.

Cover illustration: Craig Yoe
Design: Jessica Nevins

CONTENTS

CITY JOKES

The Golden Gate Bridge in San Francisco has been declared "one of the modern wonders of the world!" Nearly two miles long, it is one of the most photographed bridges in the world. The span-tastic Golden Gate was built to withstand 90-mile-per-hour winds and magnitude 8.0 earthquakes!

Golden Gate Bridge

COMEDY GOLD!

Did you hear these jokes about the Golden Gate Bridge?

No! The **SUSPENSION** is killing me!

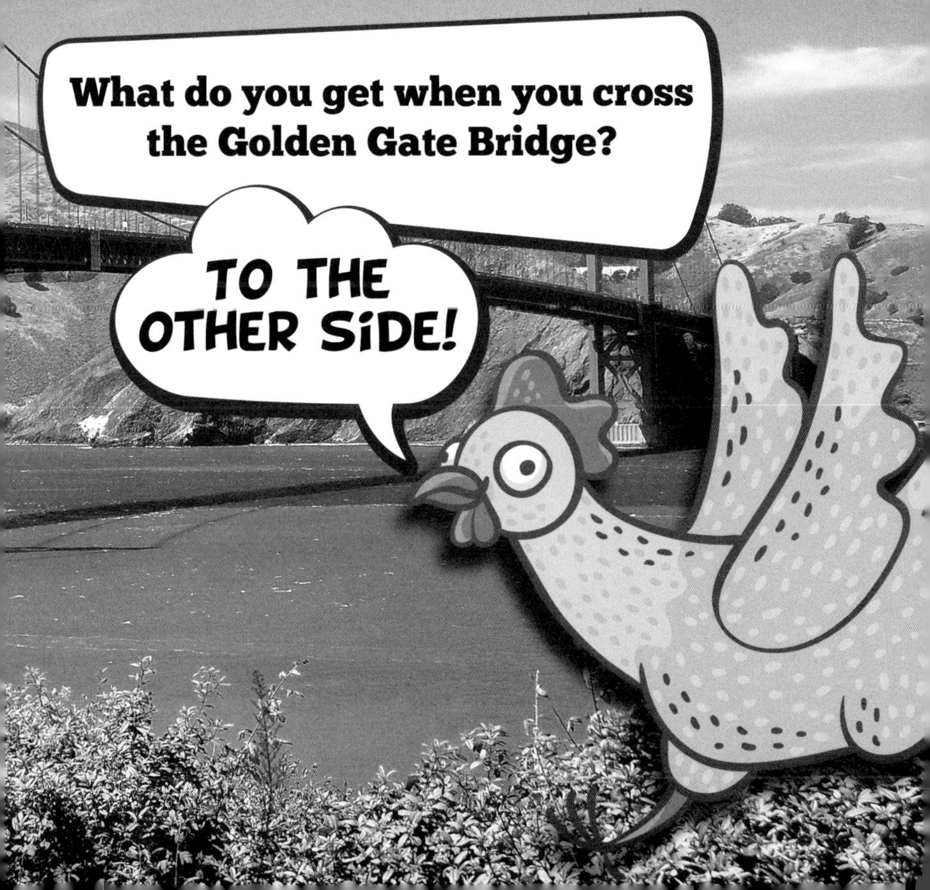

What language does the Golden Gate Bridge speak?

LOL Jokes editor:

Don't you think your Golden Gate Bridge jokes are kind of **CORNY**?

LOL Jokes writer:

Get **OVER** it!

BONUS BRIDGE FACTOID

The U.S. Navy originally planned to paint the Golden Gate Bridge with black and yellow stripes! Yipes, stripes!

NAME GAME FACTOID!

The locals will go loco if you call San Francisco these loathed names:

* Golden Gate City
* Frisco
* Fog City
* San Fran
* New York

BTW, San Francisco is named after the Catholic saint Francis of Assisi. But before it got that name it was called Yerba Buena, which is Spanish for "good herb," because of the tasty wild mint that grew in the area.

MINT-Y FRESH JOKES!

Speaking of mint, Congress established the **SAN FRANCISCO MINT** in 1852 in response to the California Gold Rush. In fact, miners needed to have their new-found gold minted into coins. Collectable coins are still made there.

A dime and a quarter were swimming in a pool. The dime jumped headfirst into the shallow end, but the quarter didn't. How come?

A HUM-DINGER FACTOID

Philadelphia may be the home of the famed **LIBERTY BELL**, but the Liberty Bell once visited San Francisco—for the Panama-Pacific International Exposition in 1915!

This Liberty Bell joke will **CRACK** you up:

A FISHY STORY!

The tourist-loved attraction and neighborhood **FISHERMAN'S WHARF** got its name for the Italian immigrant fishermen who lived there. They provided fish for prospectors coming to San Francisco during the Gold Rush.

What kind of music did the fishermen listen to?

THE WORD ON THE STREET . . . LOMBARD STREET!

Lombard Street, seen in tons of TV shows and movies, is one of the crookedest and steepest streets in the world!

Lombard Street

ROLLiNG FACTOiD

San Francisco boasts the nation's only rolling National Landmark: the city's nine-miles-per-hour beloved cable cars. Millions of human beings hop on them every year! Roll on!

POWELL & HYDE Sts.
sometimes you just need a car.
10
POWELL AND MARKET
HYDE AND BEACH
FISHERMANS WHARF
10
FISHERMANS

ALCATRAZ ANTICS

Called the toughest and scariest prison in the world, Alcatraz Federal Prison closed in 1963 and is now a popular historic site and tourist destination run by the National Park Service.

Alcatraz Island

I wanna go! How do you get to the prison?
Rob a bank!
WARNING

Why did the painting from the San Francisco Museum of Modern Art get sent to Alcatraz?

IT WAS FRAMED!

Why did the credit card serve time at Alcatraz?

It was guilty as **CHARGED!**

Yeah, but the guy who stole from Bob's Donuts was found not guilty!

LOONEY LAWS

. . . in SAN FRANCISCO!

IT'S THE LAW!

Elephants on Market Street are required to be on leashes.

In San Francisco, it's against the law to display the bodies of dead persons without their written permission.

It's a crime to bury people within the city limits.

You can be arrested for carrying bread in an open basket in San Francisco.

It is illegal in the Bay Area to walk more than nine dogs at once. **ARF! ARF!**

TELL IT TO THE JUDGE!

In San Francisco, you can't use **OLD UNDERWEAR** to wash your car.

LAWBREAKERS BEWARE!

Horse manure **CANNOT** be piled more than six feet high on San Francisco's streets.

CULTURE JOKES

DISCOVER THIS FACTOID

The Bay Area Discovery Museum (BADM) is a space for imaginations to run wild! It's located at the foot of the Golden Gate Bridge.

Where's a cow's favorite place to visit?

The Bay Area Discovery **MOO**-seum!

STUPID FACTOID

The St. Stupid's Day Parade is an annual wacky San Francisco event! Paraders behave utterly silly, wear totally ridiculous clothes, and yell incredibly stupid stuff—all to have tons o' fun for themselves and parade watchers! The St. Stupid's Day Parade is held on . . . wait for it . . . April Fool's Day!

STAR WARS NERD ALERT!

You can find a Yoda fountain in Presidio National Park, yo!

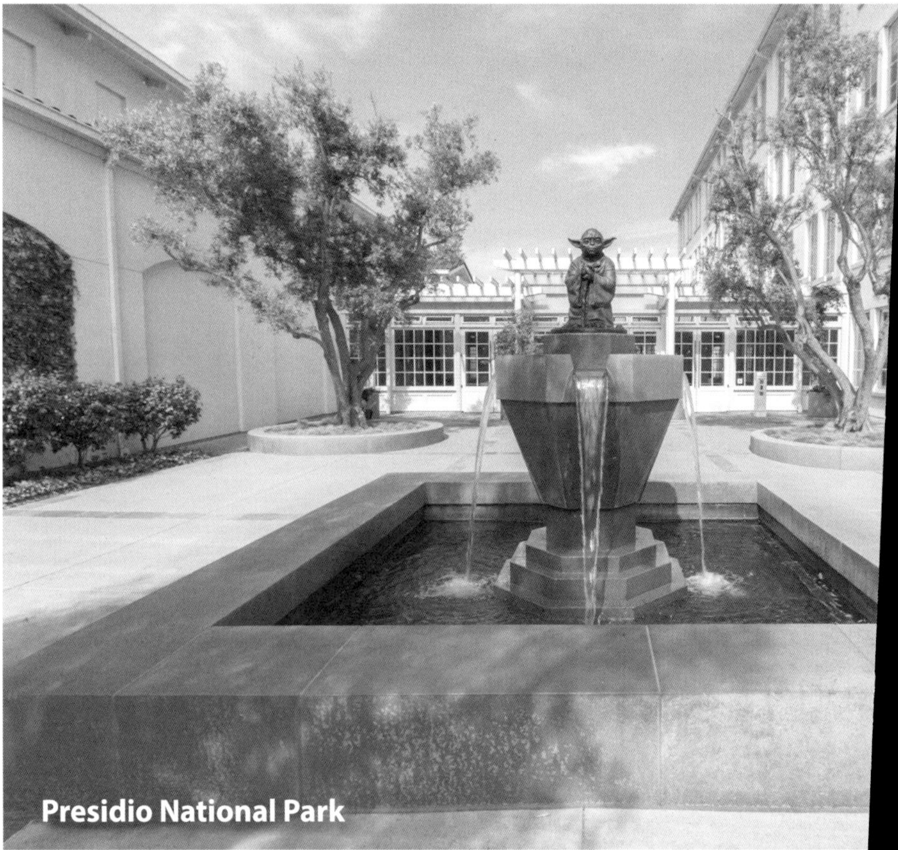

Presidio National Park

What did Yoda say to Luke when the young Jedi was struggling to eat his peas?

"Use the forks, Luke!"

LET iT BE!

The greatest rock group in history, **THE BEATLES**, played their last full concert in Candlestick Park on August 29th, 1966!

ROCK AND ROAR!

YOU'LL BE DIZZY WITH EXCITEMENT AT THE WALT DISNEY FAMILY MUSEUM!

Walt Disney Family Museum

And here are some Disney jokes to tell if you're feeling a little **GOOFY**:

Donald Daisy

Why is Cinderella so lousy at soccer?

She's always running away from the ball.

(She has a **PUMPKIN** for a **COACH**!)

STAY TOONED!

San Francisco's Cartoon Art Museum displays animation cels and the original art to comic book covers and pages. Here's some **COMIC**-al jokes you can tell there.

Why did Batman stop taking Robin fishing?
Because ROBIN kept eating all the worms!
What do you call the Hulk's potatoes?
Hulk MASHED!

CHOO-CHOO ON THIS!

The Randall Museum is the home of one of the largest model train layouts in California! These models are replicas of real trains that mobilized the Bay Area for decades.

When does a kid go just as fast as a train?

When the kid is **ON** the train!

WHAT'S A REALLY FUN PLACE TO GO?

UM, THE EXPLORATORIUM!

At the popular Exploratorium, you can see what causes earthquakes, experience a tornado, and learn ***WATT*** makes electricity work!

INSANE FACTOID

San Francisco has a museum that floats! Truth! That's the ***SEE***-worthy . . . USS *Pampanito* . . . it's a for realzies submarine!

I ate a submarine sandwich for lunch and I think I'm gonna be sick!
Why do you say that?
It's starting to SURFACE!

YOU CAN BE IN THE BEST CIRCLES!

San Francisco's **CHILDREN'S CREATIVITY MUSEUM** has a 100-year-old carousel. And you can ride it!

Children's Creativity Museum

I think I caught a cold when riding the carousel.
That's because there was something going around!

BRICK A LEG!

The Children's Creativity Museum also has the Animation Studio, where kids (and adults!) can create stop-motion animation movies—with LEGOs!

Knock-knock!
Who's there?
LEGO!
Lego who?
Lego of the door handle and let me in!

NATURE JOKES

Do you have the **FOGGiEST** idea of the answers to these fog jokes, or are you **MiST**-ified?

The crazy fog that hangs around the City by the Bay has a name:

KARL!

Hello, my name is
Karl
Did you hear the joke about Karl?
No, I MIST it!

Why did the chickens like the fog?
They love **FOWL** weather!

What's worse than a foggy day?

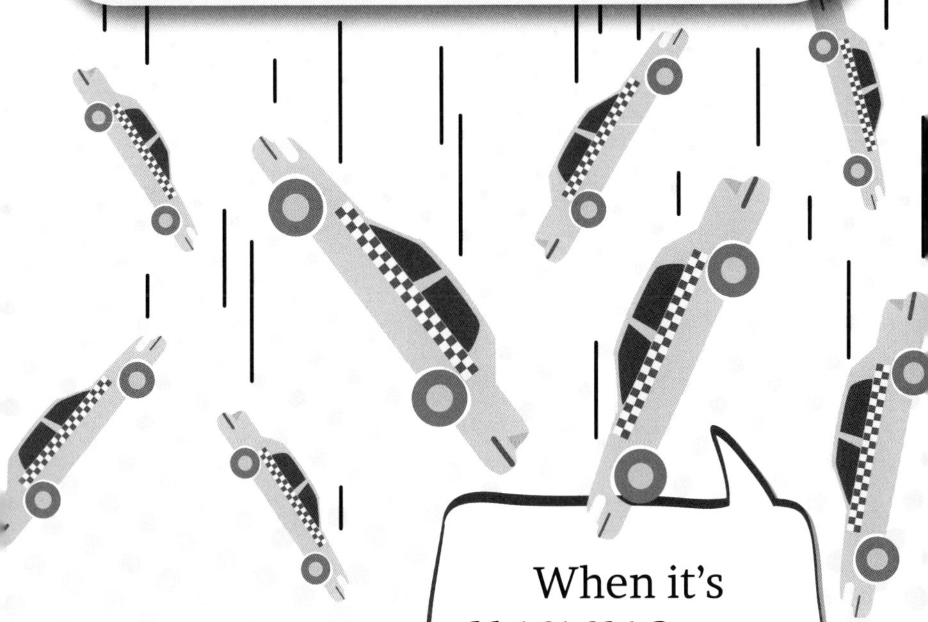

When it's **HAILING** taxis!

Did you like my fog joke?

FOG-get about it!

EARTHQ

In 1906, almost all of San Francisco was destroyed by an enormous earthquake and the devastating fires that followed.

What did the San Francisco earthquake say when it got in trouble?

It's not my FAULT!

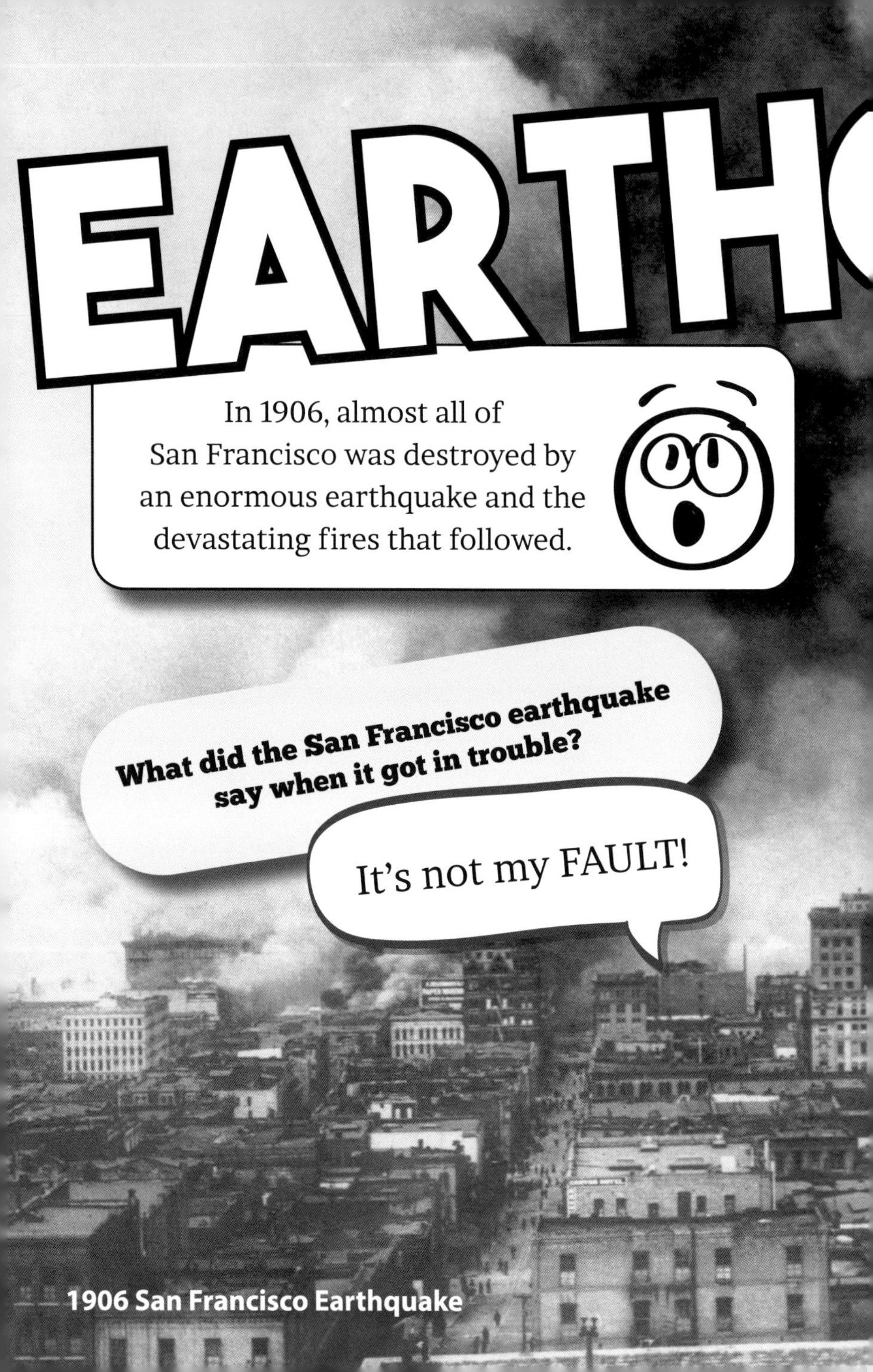

1906 San Francisco Earthquake

QUAKE!
How did the earthquake get punished?
It was GROUNDED!

YOU'LL SHAKE WITH LAUGHTER OVER THIS MIRTH-QUAKE:

What did the ground say to the earthquake?

What did the cow give after the earthquake?

SMART FACTOID

The **CALIFORNIA ACADEMY OF SCIENCES** is the most visited museum in San Francisco!

Here's some tropical humor to share while visiting the four-story rain forest at the California Academy of Sciences:

What did the South American frog mom say to her kid frog at bedtime?

ANIMAL
JOKES

BEAR WITH ME!

The bear pictured on the California state flag was modeled after a grizzly bear named **MONARCH**, who was held in captivity at Golden Gate Park, back in the late 1800s and early 1900s.

What was Monarch's favorite thing to eat?

What did they call Monarch when he got wet?

Why did the bear cross the road?
It was the chicken's day off!

What do you call bears without ears?
B's!

YOU BELONG IN A ZOO!

Go visit the 100-acre San Francisco Zoo and see **LIONS**, and **TIGERS**, and **BEARS**—OH, MY!

What has zebra stripes, giraffe spots, and pelican feathers?

The San Francisco Zoo! Wild!

ROSES ARE RED
VIOLETS ARE BLUE
I SAW A FACE LIKE YOURS
AT THE
SAN FRANCISCO ZOO!

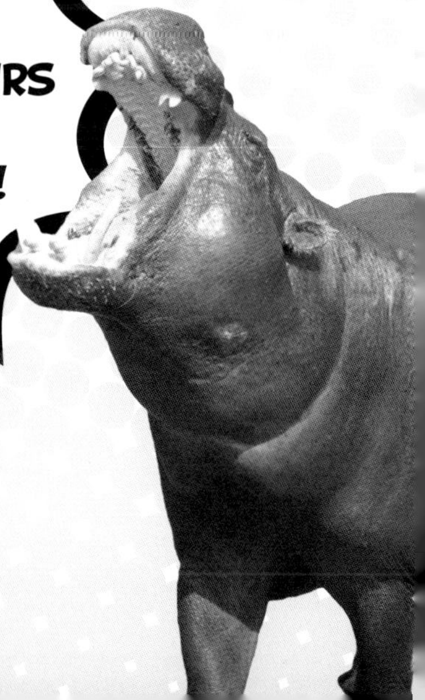

THE BAY AREA HAS A PET CEMETERY! DOG GONE!

Founded in the 1950s, the Presidio Pet Cemetery is located under the Route 101 overpass. It is the final resting place of 400 gone-but-not-forgotten pets.

Why do they build fences around cemeteries?

<DRUM ROLL>

FEARSOME FiSH FACTOiD

This may sound fishy, but at the Aquarium of the Bay you can actually touch a starfish, a stingray, and a . . . BABY SHARK!

Which fish at the aquarium is the most famous?

THE STAR FiSH!

What sea creature at the Aquarium of the Bay can wave "hi" eight times at once?

What does a baby shark eat for lunch?

POLLY WANTS A CRACK-UP!

If you keep your eyeballs peeled, you can spot a huge flock of South American parrots flying around Telegraph Hill—nobody is sure how they got there.

What do they call seagulls in San Francisco?

FOOD JOKES

DONUT MISS THIS!

San Francisco's Bob's Donuts sells a donut the size of a human head! If you eat the Big One in under two minutes, Bob's will refund your money, give you a free drink and t-shirt, and list you in the Bob's Hall of Fame!

Half-baked Factoid: Bob's has a location on **BAKER** Street!

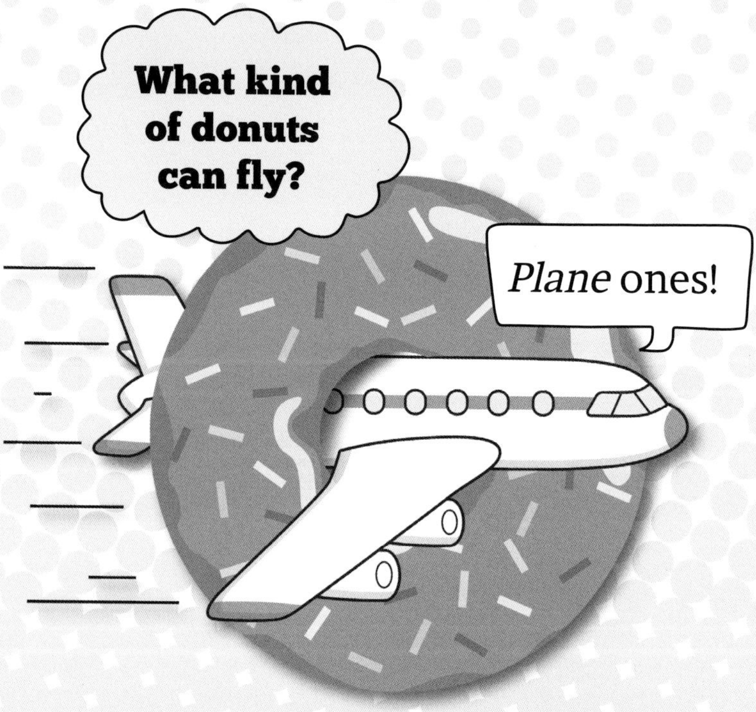

Why do golfers like Bob's donuts?

What do you call someone who makes donuts in San Francisco?

Why did the donut go to the dentist?

BOFFO BURRITOS and their CORNY JOKES!

San Francisco's Mission Street is where you can find many nationally acclaimed burrito shops! DROOL!

What did the taco say when he saw his friend the burrito?

And when he said goodbye?

What's a snowman's favorite Mexican food?

And a cat's fave?

I SEE A VISIT TO A FORTUNE COOKIE FACTORY IN YOUR FUTURE!

In the 1890s, Makoto Hagiwara, a Japanese resident of San Francisco, had the **GOOD FORTUNE** of thinking up the Chinese fortune cookie! And now your fam can get a tour of the Golden Gate Fortune Cookie Factory in Chinatown!

Here are some of the funniest actual fortunes that have been found in fortune cookies:

"I'm glad to escape that cookie!"

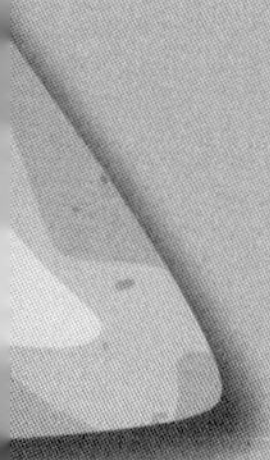

"I cannot help you,
for I am just a cookie!"

"Congrats, you can read!"

"I see money in your future—
it's not yours, though."

"I can't believe you are
about to eat my tiny home."

"Help! I'm being held prisoner
in a cookie factory!"

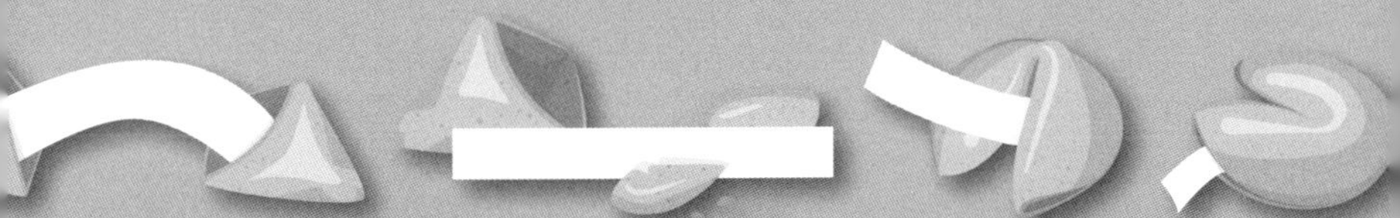

SPORTS JOKES

RUNNING JOKES!

Bay to Breakers is the longest-running annual footrace in the world. Ready, set, GO! This event, which started in 1912, begins at the Embarcadero and runs over seven miles to Ocean Beach. The wacky part is that all the runners wear crazy cool costumes and some wear nothing at all!

Did you hear about the lettuce and the tomato who were racing to a burrito?
JOG my memory!
The lettuce was aHEAD and the tomato was trying to KETCH-UP!
Did you hear about the waves that raced to Ocean Beach?
Is this a running gag?
Yeah, they were *tide*!

SPORT-Y JOKES!

What has 18 legs and catches flies?

The Oakland Athletics!

Why is the weather so cool in San Francisco?

Why did the defensive player for the San Jose Earthquakes cross the road?

Why couldn't the Golden State Warrior go on vacation?

Do you know what the enforcer on the San Jose Sharks does?

Yes, of course!

Just checking!

WHAT DID THE 49ER SAY TO THE FOOTBALL?

"CATCH YA LATER!"